## BOOKS BY RICARDO PAU-LLOSA

*Sorting Metaphors*
*Bread of the Imagined*
*Cuba*
*Vereda Tropical*
*The Mastery Impulse*
*Parable Hunter*
*Man*

# Ricardo Pau-Llosa

Carnegie Mellon University Press
Pittsburgh 2014

## ACKNOWLEDGMENTS

Grateful acknowledgment is made of the magazines where many of these poems first appeared:

*Alaska Quarterly Review*: "Amazing Grace Man"
*Ambit*: "Absolution Man," "Little Dog Man"
*The American Poetry Review*: "Give-Us-This-Day Man"
*Bateau*: "Milk and Honey Man," "Fool-for, Slave-for Man," "Calling Disciples Man"
*Bayou*: "Leper-No-More Man"
*Beloit Poetry Journal*: "Bethany Man"
*Birmingham Poetry Review*: "God-Is-Love Man"
*Caliban*: "Sophia Man," "Lion's Den Man"
*Cold Mountain Review*: "Gerasene Man"
*Crab Orchard Review*: "Micah Man"
*Cream City Review*: "Venial Sins Man"
*Cuadernos de ALDEEU*: "Grail Man," "Cardinal Sins Man"
*December*: "Patmos Man," "Healer Man"
*Diagram*: "Agape Man"
*Faultline*: "Scourging-at-the-Pillar Man"
*The Fiddlehead*: "Pontius Pilate Man," "Hands-in-the-Wounds Man"
*Fourteen Hills*: "Giant Slayer Man"
*Image*: "Original Sin Man," "Confirmation Man"
*Interim*: "Gethsemane Man," "Elijah Man"
*Kenyon Review* (online): "Nicodemus Man"
*Kestrel*: "Extreme Unction Man," "Dead Sea Man"
*Margie*: "Vestal Virgin Man"
*Midwest Quarterly*: "Cave-of-Jeremiah Man"
*Natural Bridge*: "Empty Tomb Man"
*New England Review*: "Lazarus Man," "Cana Man"
*North American Review*: "Eucharist Man"
*Poetry*: "Monstrance Man"
*Poetry Salzburg Review*: "Adultery Man," "Last Supper Man"
*Rhino*: "Matrimony Man"
*Rock & Sling*: "Chalice Man," God-Is-Truth Man," "Turn-the-Other-Cheek Man"
*Salmagundi*: "Epic Man"
*Spoon River Poetry Journal*: "Conversion Man"
*Stand*: "Crucifixion Man," "Caiaphas Man," "Holy Orders Man," "Broken Seals Man"

Book design by Cole Heiner

Library of Congress Control Number 2013937135
ISBN 978-0-88748-584-8
Printed and bound in the United States of America
10 9 8 7 6 5 4 3 2 1

# CONTENTS

*In memory of Ana Rosa Nuñez, and to Ron De Maris,*
*poets and mentors, for their generosity of spirit*

*Woe to those who call evil good*
*and good evil,*
*who put darkness for light*
*and light for darkness,*
*who put bitter for sweet*
*and sweet for bitter.*

—Isaiah 5:20

# EASTER MAN

He was the egg they laid,
his parents meant, saying
instead, You were an accident,

so be careful when you go out,
now that you must. The skirts
flutter, we know that, the rouge dawns.

And slave you must be to all that.
Like a house-closing, so the new
owner could feel legal

and not herself a slave to biting
need, to bruise and tangle.
For who would accept the governance

of flesh, that rickety bridge
over tooth-cut foam,
in the passed-out forest,

in their right mind
or their left, snoring
in the dank corners

where forgotten luggage roosts,
in the hangar—the last thing
they saw of home.

## BAPTISM MAN

He hoses the lawn and the potted plants—
the purple blooms, the red ones,
forgot their names so makes up new ones.

The red-butterfly catcher,
the moth motel bush,
the humming bird seducer.

The broad-winged hat
helmets his shadow on the patio,
so he feels armed against the sun.

He conquers drizzly. The bugs
lift when he sprays their homes,
and the toads croak indignant

they hadn't sensed the shower coming.
Their skins smell the air for storm,
but he renders sense useless.

Those are the instincts of a past world.
It is drought time and he is the water god.
With thirty minutes before he has to shower

and dress and get to work, half the yard
must wait for sunset. Half the toads
keep themselves. Half the bugs sleep rightly.

## ABSOLUTION MAN

The man wondered why the three women he had loved
dreamt about having a penis. He certainly had no desire
or entertained illusions or otherwise speculated,
in whatever alien moments of escape from oneself,
however vaporous and susceptible to being explained
by a turn in eating habits or a martini buzz,
what it might be like to have a vagina.

And why bring it up, in bed say, after the fourth
gorging of a seminal night? I had a dream, dear,
in which I was a man pissing at a urinal.
Yes, we do that, he would grumble dozing off.
That's us, at urinals. And he'd fall off into deep sleep
not grateful that the last word from that blissful state
to usher him into a paradisiacal appraisal
of what had just transpired was the word urinal.

His busy mind got to work. Let's edit, it would say,
as he slumped into the pillow of earned numbness.
Uranus. Let that be the word. The planet, not the pun.
OK, Quirinale, the hill in Rome, imperial, abusive,
lethargic at the very end but still elegant in laurel
and purple. Too convoluted. What is the word,
what is the word with which we bid adieu
to one finished chapter of the world that we might
think ourselves the authors of the next?

# EUCHARIST MAN

After hammering nails for three decades
on walls increasingly cramped, so now
barely an inch frontiers paintings,

he can stop thinking about slamming
his thumb or smashing his lenses.
He is good at this vice, this gardening

of what fellow artists have abandoned
to sale. O, one or two have said, you
have that piece. I had forgotten. . . .

The hoarder never forgets
for he is not stashing trophies
of the hunt but the facets

of a fly's lens who peer inward
and he back at them, and nowhere
can he hide from what cannot help

but look at him. No jewel box
whose pendants chime the obscure,
no panoply of awe for citizens,

drinks in hand, nodding or disnodding
this or that acquisition. The hoarder
is the deserted island, art his loyal surf.

## CONFIRMATION MAN

And who looks like his passport photo,
may I ask? The man often lost his cool
at immigration counters and customs
and wherever documents met metaphors
of the frailty of life. Look carefully,
officer, behold what a little less beard
has done for youthfulness overflowing
from a face no torment could mar?

Yes, I see, officer, you too are a pensive man,
furrowed brow, dimming eyes, the waste
of it all scooping into a tremble only you
can sense long before others will stare away
at empty space or idiotic signs so as not
to be detectively rude. The great appetite is always

hungry for us who meal away on wilting trays
called lines, at banks, theaters, or here, officer.
This too is a way to ascertain how little it matters
that one looks the part or parts one's hair
differently. I am the camouflage, maestro
of the badged entreaty. I am the one
trying to get away with murder, my own.

## MATRIMONY MAN

When he learned to cook, for solvency's sake,
he began with crepes. No staples. No meat.
Make sure the skillet is hot and the oil

turns within itself in little bitten lips.
Then the mix of egg and milk and flour
pours into the desired moon.

And the edges need dabs of oil,
and they brown and the surface bubbles
and gels, and it is then, he tells

the invisible apprentice who stands
for him when he stood by his grandmother,
it is then you flip the crepe. I am calling

it a crepe because you, heir to my skills,
are from this land. She and I called them
freichuelos. From Asturias Celtic hungers.

That's the sun and moon of it.
I married no one, he is ready to admit,
yet here are my children, forks in hand,

napkins flapping from their necks
like mating lizards in his yard.
He sits at her table. One plate. One glass.

# HOLY ORDERS MAN

Finally, when he broke down
and paid for it, the dream
he'd been having

of Tarzan and the Missionary Nun
became a reality. For an hour, OK,
but a reality. The woman charged

extra to wear the rented habit
and pretend to pray demurely
as he, in faux leather briefs,

would ask her, Lost again
in my jungle, Sister? She shuddered
preferring the trite collar-and-lash

number of her other clients.
She wasn't into new liturgy,
he could tell. A traditionalist,

which made her deflowering
all the more arousing, he being
such a rebel, throwing off

the chains that had kept him
in dreams for so many ledgers
and two and a half marriages.

# EXTREME UNCTION MAN

For once, he would have loved
not to have sauce all over his shirt.
Even when the meal was dryer

than a dog biscuit, he would manage
to action-paint his Polo. This one time
he thought about tempting the gods

of sauce and gravity,
and would take this new woman
to a Mexican restaurant way out

of town, far from his townhouse
so he couldn't just make a quick dash home
to change and catch that movie.

No, this time, he figured,
the jinx could only be broken
with courage, downright, bib-less

courage. Her online profile
prompted him for daring
and overcoming fears, and warned

against smokers and slobs.
He'd win her with a tightrope burrito
above a guacamole net.

# VENIAL SINS MAN

The slender academician in a long cotton dress
and flowing eyes calls for volunteers to sit in the lobby
and tell her laptop the oral contortions of home,

the felt concept, the actual shed, the childhood winnowed
from textbooks on trauma. He'll make it up, he figures,
as he sits dodging onerous drowsy bellhops

and ill-hatted tourists, for this project is important enough
for a grant. The very notion of region will be framed,
subtexted and glossed. He confesses, I don't have a home.

O no, her dimming wrinkled eyelids say,
another one who bungee-corded into Beckett River.
And why not, little one? her silence asks,

her arm right-angled to the table behind the screen
that screens them from each other below the nose ridge.
The man asks himself these questions all the time,

puts them in bubbles above nice people's heads.
I have an epic sense of life, he sombers forth. Which means?
Doesn't know right off. Well, he blurts, like Aeneas in love

with horizons that are worth the trouble, even if he will never
harvest the rewards. Americans have lost that, he says,
weapon of exile in hand. Is this thing on? No, she says.

# EPIC MAN

*for David W. Brubeck*

Eat almonds before you go to bed,
his best friend admonished him,
and you'll feel the energy of the good fat
in the morning. O to become
the Mandorla Man. He overlaps alright,
like postage stamps—paper on paper
with the glue that sends the envelope on.

His best friend plays the trombone,
composes for the trunk
of this one-note instrument
the melodious maze. Art cannot die,
they tell themselves over scotch
and brandy and cigars.
Read me a poem,
his breathless-from-five-pieces
friend begs.

Here's one about my trip to the Amazons,
sitting in a dugout canoe, one of a dozen beans
on this wooden string, all of us vested
with orange odes to the life we cling to
white-knuckled. This rock on the shore,
this tree where the guide knows the river will bend—
they aren't the piercing heraldry.
We artists are the water bobbing

beneath the splintered asses, knocking
those who hate the clock of life
but love time into the seedling grave.
Even if we tip over and drown
in the Coca-Cola waters, covered
in tick-like bugs called *niguas*

that dig into your flesh and breed
forever and ever, we are art.
History is the account and we the checks
that never bounce. The friend
opens a spigot at the end
of the long brass river
to shake the spittle out,
the blood of the played music,
clear and sparkling.

Whoever invented baptism
understood the poem of water—
I see that now
that the ecotourists giggle with savage water
all over their faces and clothes. Bestowed.
Like them, it will dry.

And that painting over there,
the friend says, lungs calm
with old air again. It's by a naif
painter from another jungle-haunted
place. Ricardo Avila of Costa Rica.
It's a picture of Venice,
the Grand Canal, and it's snowing
on the Piazza. The lion and his column tilt,
and his wings tilt, and the dome, everything
has a melt about it in the cottony air.
As if the artist had fallen out
of the gondola and peered
up and hopefully from one arc of the nut
to the other where the world
ticks but doesn't stop talking.

# VESTAL VIRGIN MAN

Legal's legal. She turns 18 at midnight.
18 turned on me ten years ago, or thereabouts.
The point is that I am not her dad.
I only talk to myself about these matters
because you never know who else to trust.

You should have seen how she ate
the sumptuous, irrepressible, overstuffed
squid at the restaurant, its ink
pooling into a dark bed on the creamy
porcelain, the cherry red peppers
languid at the saucy edges.

And how she walked and neared
and took my arm in the fake winter
of Lincoln Road, her almost nothing
of a skirt flapping like a rolodex.
I would glimpse her ass abovingly,
accidental fred-n-gingers locking time,
but surely the waiters and the salesmen
at the passing bistros got the better view.

Later was later. It was everything
those beery thugs at the breezy tables
might have imagined. It was everything.
I'd say You should have been there,
but I'm glad you weren't.
You overheard me tell her,
We're on Lincoln Road, Babe,
so get ready for some emancipation.
You like that, eh? Bad jokes always work,
that's why there aren't any.

# CRUCIFIXION MAN

Why, he wonders, is sushi so expensive
when they don't even have to cook the stuff?
Every restaurant is a feverish abacus
hedging spoilage and fuel and square inches
of seating and penny-variants of napkin styles.
If you dim the lights, do the customers
eat more, less, the same? Save on bulbs.
Drinks go up? Tips go down?

Calculus ignores the life it reasons
because you have to love the symbols
to get them. The man always botched
anything that had to with numbers,
dense aquatic of the wordy trenches.
It's not like he wound up with art
and poems because he made a wrong turn
as a waiter and betrayed this destiny,

that of restaurateur par excellence.
What numberless choice but to wind up
on this bus stop flipping through the sushi menu
someone had left there, or had blown
off a windshield or slipped
indecorously from a thrown newspaper,
or like a message from the proverbial bottle
or the maligned texts of old,
to run itself aground in his open palms,
to be pondered for the price
if not the taste or sustenance
of that other life he gulped down
once like a dry wafer?

# TURN-THE-OTHER-CHEEK MAN

The man decides to give his writing class
an impromptu assignment sticky
with existentialism. Suppose cellular biologists
have discovered how to stop aging
by doing this or that to mitochondria,
and everyone born after a certain date
need not worry about dying—of old age, at least.
They can still be crushed by a truck,
or have their throats cut, or catch a disease.
But they won't age so, technically, they just
might live forever. The man looks
back down from the walls that dissolved
as he imagined this freedom-vanquished world
and panned the room full of students,
frozen like tattoos, unable to muster
the pretense of an interest.
This is for a grade, folks, he warns them,
so they take notes. Now, he says,
let's say by some stroke of really bad luck
this mitochondrial treatment misses you
by a few months, weeks, days even.
Had you been born three days earlier
you would never die. Alas, you will
flab and leather and cough into the gray
abyss which has been humanity's lot.
Those just a bit younger than you
are safe and see you differently,
leprously perhaps, compassionately
after a few drinks, for they can't imagine
the bitterness a knife's date has signed
upon your flesh or how it's dumped you
like an Alka Seltzer into a glass of water

and turned you into the bubbling clock
we all were once. So, tell me in five hundred words,
with a clearly established thesis statement
in the introductory paragraph, supporting
facts, rhetorical diversity, logical and clear
movement of ideas, just how it feels to know
you will be the last of your kind to hate
time and mirror and looming retirement.
Or maybe there is some joy in old destinies,
a freedom to live on edges your mitochondrial
friends will not venture near, for how great
would their loss be if the parachute did not open,
or the horse reared, or the wine goblet
was dirty with indivisible daggers.
Some would miser themselves into shut rooms,
for now that they know what to fear
they are consecrated to feel nothing else.
You whom no science could hope
might just be willing to be joyous
that this little life can only be filled
by compression. They stare back at him
in the air-conditioned hum.
One asks, You mean, like my friends
stay young and I turn into. . . .
You turn into me, says the man
to save him from the cliff of a courteous pause.
O my God! gasps the young man
as if trapped in the eye of a needle.

## CHALICE MAN

He walks for an hour a day,
three miles, in arch-supporting shoes,
donning the new stainless sunblock,
swinging his arms to get the heart
right, no cell phone, listening
to the crunch of his step
over gravel or dry leaf,
the rumble of car, and glints
past the upheavaled dust
to delight in the jaw-bent
soda can the hour has silvered,
and for all his zen
he is content to also trench inward
and scoop down the yearnings
and scoop up the triumphs,
and hope they balance out
the way what's left of a fluid
coating the cup is pulled
to the bottom by the earth
because that is where
the patient and the tired
must equally come to halo.

# LAST SUPPER MAN

What else can the man who collects all this art do
but give parties? Some are dinners, some gather
the tumbling tribe in scotches and canapés.
The guests have been brought here, not to see
what the man has so earnestly and discerningly
picked from a world of pages of images
fluttering through the fevers of studios,
beasts really freed from the easel's cage
and onto the free plains of the man's walls
on which they can roam into minds.
No, they have been called here to be in the midst.
Free to look, they stand instead with drinks
in hand, chortle and gossip and flirt.
The man knows the weight of stubbornness
earns no helper to carry it. He is like a beekeeper
who gives buckets of honey to his friends,
to all of them. Even to the diabetic ones,
to the ones who'd rather suck mud than honey.
You there, allergic? Well, then, take another bucket.
What do you mean, I shouldn't have?
If you don't take the bucket, all I have left
is the buzz and the sting and the odd
contraptions all over the field
between the trees whose flowers
will soon turn to solemn fruit.

# CARDINAL SINS MAN

When parking meters are broken,
a virgule-slashed capital P
flashes its directive on the little screen:
No Parking. More than absurd,
it is vanity, for had the meter been
in working order and willing
to glutton his quarters,
then he would be spared the rage
born of this indignity, looking around,
feeling ridiculous questioning himself—
Should I spineless obey and move my car
or leave it there in this perfectly good space?
It is not the space that is out of order
but the state's ability to collect tribute.
A Mercedes has pulled up close
in tints, chatting on a phone, grinning,
guessing the man is pondering
what to do. That greedy Mercedes,
thinks the man, lusting after his space,
waiting to see what good citizenry
will bequeath him. He is torn,
but the scale is tipped by the CEO shine,
and the man slouches off on foot, his face
dished to the ground as if receiving
signals from the pavement. Look at that,
the grin behind the tints must be thinking,
that bum's too cheap to find another space,
too lazy to give up what he should.

## MONSTRANCE MAN

As a boy he had trouble speaking,
past three before a real word preened
from his lips. And for the longest time,
malaprops haunted him. His older sister
did what she could to train the bitten seal
of his brain to twirl the red ball
on the nose of eloquence, and his grandmother
tired of insisting he utter the names
of toys or foods—for every desire
was coded—and gave him whatever
he grunted and pointed to.
O, the man then a boy
thought, when I tower among them
I should invent my own speech
and leave others empty and afraid
that they did not know it, could not ask
or plead their case in the one tongue
that mattered. I shall have them
look upon the simplest things,
the man then a boy thought,
and fill up with stolen awe,
and point with their faces,
their pupils wide as blackened coins,
and hope with all the revenue
shattered heart-glass can muster
that someone had grasped
their need as need and not
as the monstrous coupling
of sounds in a trance of whims.
Then, the grind of his teeth
vowed, then the plazas of my city
will fill with my name,
and their blood will matter
as little to them as to me.

# MONK MAN

The names people give to things—
television, clown fish—to cite just two.
From afar, the vision has come,
now that's clever, thought the man
in one of those moods he often took on
like a doughnut break in a rigorous diet.
How silly, he thought, because everything
today was going to be silly-damned,
names especially. A fish decorated
to meld with coral suddenly becomes a clown.
What's funny about camouflage?
Life and death, for godsake. Life and death.
In his aquarium, they shot here and there,
in and out of plastic caves and the harp
of bubbles that kept the sentence of water
and acids and lights in balance,
so the fish could punctuate the dark room
with their striped peculiars,
orange and white. And he pondered
the pages of his hours in a boxed sea.
Like the barricades, he thought.
Orange and white. Why not call them
the barricade fish? Or two-tone shoes,
or éclair fish, they who seem binary
and look the same near or far?

# HOLY WATER MAN

Spring and drought in Miami.
A city by a swamp, surrounded
by sea and lakes, can't figure
how to net the harvest of hurricanes
and summer drenchers,
like Joseph and his cows.
Or pharaoh's cows,
or those in his dream
sulking in his river,
for it was his alright,
all of it, Nile and sand
and the papyrus the man
has planted by his driveway
and swayed begging him
to risk the fine and anoint them.
I have brought you onto a land
that cannot see itself in its element,
the man wanted to say
to his papyrus reeds
sanding in thirst, buoyant
in the cradle of a sunny breeze.
But his beloved plants
must have known that the man
was himself a vat of liquid
made flesh, and if he were
squeezed or smoked
he'd give off 170 of his 200 lbs
in steam or water,
and if he would only just
sweat a little over them,
or piss on them,
that might just do it,

or cry a little, or spit.
Spit on us who love you,
that we might live to hate as well.

# LION'S DEN MAN

At 51 the man buried his grandmother,
no funeral, so his mother received
respectful visitors all that week
in his living room. He sat quietly,
as he did as a child when grown-ups
preferred to yak for hours, shuffling
the epic stabs of exile—firing squads
and tortures back home—with gossip's
mothy wing dust and fashion scans.
He stared from the marbled plastic beach ball
of his deepest mind speechless
as his mother conversed with the visiting
lady, struck at the same mint of mind
in the same tropic place, paged
into the glacier of a baroque mirror.
Mutely still as a brook stone grown moon-like,
half always osseous in the solar wash
and half murked in the fungal night,
he could not catch so much as the sound
of his own breath in the magnetic poles
of his ears to scrawl down the sky
of this opal moment. He sank
undeservedly stunned that nothing had changed
in the props, cues, script and lights
on the hollow stage of Cuban conversation
where monologues dueled and no one heard a thing
the other said, for there was but one person
in the audience, and he was a child, legs swinging
beneath the velvet cliff of a creaky chair.

# LAZARUS MAN

What if he lost the lotto ticket?
The man worries about such things.
And what if he couldn't bring himself
to look at the winning numbers that week,
dreading they might have been his,
but he didn't know his numbers,
because he lets the machine pick them,
so what's the problem, really?
He'd never know if he had won or lost,
or if the winner was some hapless idiot
who found his ticket on the floor
of the pharmacy next to the condoms.
But the man would know the dread
of having won and lost, and for that
he didn't need the parade of witness.
He'd walk around the rest
of his unpardoned life never
trying his luck or letting anyone
ask him, What would you do if you won?
He'd keep a corpse-tight lip
on what only he had been chosen to live.

# CANA MAN

It was the guests who act like children,
barking at him when he couldn't find
the music they wanted to hear,
or climbing on top of each other
on the delicate chair for a slobbering kiss.
They who growled at the waitress earlier
at the bar because she wasn't bringing
the drinks fast enough. What to do
with these people, the man asked himself,
now that I invited them into my house,
now that I must live among them?
Life had quagmired him in Miami,
the land of designer boors. Or had he
strapped the sandbags onto his ankles
and hurled himself into the din of place,
chanting cause-duties and fake nobilities
to himself alone now with the Ids
who want another change of music,
and peanuts, and cheese, and rifle
his cabinets demanding, demanding.
Water is water. Wine is wine.

## SOPHIA MAN

All bright people
start dim in adolescence,
wringing their mental hands
over the color Blue.
*Is blue for me blue for you?*
the promising lad would ask
himself and the grin of priests
trained to sniff the egg crack
of philosophy. Much later
he could say with aplomb,
Camouflage is for philosophers
who entertain
the contaminations of mind to mind.
Of course, he felt and downright planned
the need to explain, to that semiotics
major the night he read his poems
in Savannah, he 29 and she 19.
The blue of this obnoxious dress,
he said taking the silken strap
between the coin of his fingers,
will always be private to us,
but look, my dear, at lizards and octopi,
praying mantises and other traffickers
in seem, how they condone
the common anchor of form.
They fool all our eyes
and those of appetite and refuge
equally enough to spell a certainty
and haunt proposal—that we can attain
the Ion's link. Interpreter is electric,
my dear, like this blue
I so wish you too would wish to lose.

# GIANT SLAYER MAN

Rifling brochures
of day tours to whale tails
dipping or towers ivying
reconfirmed the collective
myriad meaningless.
It was that slingshot
that slew him onto a life
whose rocks he turned to find
other rocks. Nowhere
was guardianship, nor happily
did love or friend linger
pompously long
so as to accuse
this egg timer of subtleties.
No briefs or rebuttals.
He wandered
in mind the countries
he had no bread to travel,
in page after merciless page
that cut into this fingertips.
Little purses of tornness
where he could sock away
the howling chalk-drawn suckling.
Let another, crossing
the world with a life bundled,
here and there glimpse
the outline of lust on a pane
to feel the promised landing.

# LITTLE DOG MAN

The scene was more sickening than the time
the man stuffed himself with stale popcorn,

mesmerized by that nature show episode
where the gray whale mother tries

to outswim a pack of killer whales hunting her calf,
betting on her size to keep the newborn close,

to no avail finally, as the black and white
of it descended like card sharks on its tongue.

That was all they wanted, a little tongue
ripped out of the drowned youth

in sight of the mother pregnant
with the grief of a broken mission

and who would have gladly given herself
to the killers the ocean, her god, had sent.

And when the orcas, belly bright,
flew off from their short feast in arcs and coils,

the mother followed the comma of her flesh,
certain of its numbness, followed it

until it sank past her depth, caught
its last lights like a pale kerchief, read

the last echo drummed back from its shell,
and saw it become an ever tinier host

set in the monstrance of that darkness
where a penury of scavengers awaited

leadened by the night familiar, who rest there
in the morgue delectable of jeweled vermin

grateful for the rare appetites of a higher world,
that diners should leave not crumbs and bones

but a beast that would fill a calendar of ambition
and make golden the held breath of solid night.

# DEAD SEA MAN

Write it out of you, the man's friends advised,
that vile woman, it's your survival strategy—
how fortunate you writers are that way.
But, the man said, she had been the flimsy raft
that bounced by when my arms were about to give out,
only to fray with the hump of waves and pour me
back into the marble of the sea. So, the friends said,
swim for it, now that the raft gave you respite—
why, look, there's the shore! But, the man begged,
I had labored night and day to repair the raft,
turn it into a sailboat with my shirt,
whittled it a liner's bow with my knife.
O, the counselors hummed with chin strokes,
scraping the reef, finally, of a wisdom
about the man they had resisted.
You were the raft's raft,
only rafts don't need saving.
They yearn to dissolve in the open sea
where only trash haloes the surface. Always
the waves, a shore, the imagined strength of arms.

# ASK-AND-YOU-SHALL-RECEIVE MAN

The man slumps alone on a cement slab
in the college plaza where the night
students forage for junk food.

A woman in lavender scrubs
bangs on the machine that dispenses
chips and cookies, next to the soda pop

and the protein drinks, and she hopes
her fist will make the chip bag
trapped in the dented spiral

fall into the belly with the snap door
from where she can retrieve
what she paid for, although the ghost

on the glass that pounds back at her
is angry she has stirred the god of fairness
from the bliss of indifferent sleep.

# GRAIL MAN

The man chopsticks ice cubes
in his Dewar's with two black stirs
and watches how they dip
in their sleek amber veritas
to rise again more less than more.
Cubes like belugas
wheeling into the sea,
spacecraft or meteors
souped in a galactic honey
junkyard of free slipperies.
He knows the delight
of entertaining impossibles
as he gestures his fingers to seize
the jelly-lit gems, the fat coins
of cold teeth ducking
into this corneal pond.
Trapped yet derisive of solids—
the way the plot of his marriage
slumps into the lava
of that sea, memory,
enamored with itself.

# EMPTY TOMB MAN

This eviction notice was unusually polite
yet fragrant with firmness.
It begged the debtor to have compassion
on those who cannot show any.
It made references to the seasons—
how the effect spring must follow
the cause winter—and on it bloomed,
in computer cursive, the date
of unenviable departure.
The man was moved
but did not know to what, or where
really, because the order
to physically vacate
was now preambled with spirit
jostling prose, promises
of nature's curative stubbornness,
and other lures to align
world and hope which,
had the man's wife too been possessed
by the saving style of the notice,
it might have turned their final breakup
into a flower bed, instead
of a burning crater whose one
lidless eye pulled heaven
down, down into the ravenous
gut of grief.

# GERASENE MAN

Band-Aids is what the man missed most
about America when he traveled
across Latin America, pursuing art and women,
the fleeting curdling of the pudding life.
When he cut his finger or his face shaving,
and he had forgotten to pack those Band-Aids,
he had to settle for the poorly sticking
local imitations of imperial health. Custom,
comfort, how these yearnings trickle forth
from the scrapes of existence. Then the man
one day fell in love with a woman
and lived with her in her city in her ways,
in what first seemed luxury. Then,
that day the elevator stalled,
or the bout with those unrefrigerated eggs,
and the near mugging and the constant traffic jams,
and the sheer poorness of even his servant-coiffed life
wore at him, tore so that his joy seemed
like a burning wound that would not suffer
healing, and nakedness threw him
to the soul's dank ground,
and this just wasn't love, was it? His screams
spat out of him like frantic pigs racing
toward the prodigal cliffs of home.

# HEALER MAN

Plodding along highways, the man
always congratulated himself
over resisting the youthful desire
to become a tollbooth operator. The ease
of sitting there, giving change, mumbling
directions to bleary tourist. Youth is so
indelicate a landscape of false strengths,
the man had also guarded against other torpors
of that night of beginnings—women
whose poison others dredged,
jobs that soon led to boredom's chisel.
What had shepherded him—he wondered
on this drizzly autumn drive from a failed
first date after his wife finally left him—
toward a rummaged peace with himself?
What immortal hand had swindled symmetry
from the chaos so verdantly overrunning
the lives of friends? Whatever it was,
he thought to the anvil of the wipers,
it chose carefully what parts of a soul to heal
and which to leave in the cradle and parapet
of earned hell. As it did with the bodies of others—
the liver cured but not the eye or skin. Or the skin now
lustrous, the tooth forgiven, the eye spared,
but the leg must stay bent, the mind unsprung.
In like manner, did the chooser forage
among the cherishings in his attic spirit?
The man finally understood
a moment's passing through miracle,
a coin drop wherein the team of flesh is made
to start again though partial, wounded,
aimed slumberingly at the visible road.

# PONTIUS PILATE MAN

The 10th grade chemistry teacher
illustrated the miraculous fooling
of hands on the theme
of temperature, making students
put one hand in hot water
and the other in cold so that alternately
dipping them in a lukewarm tub
spoke different truths to each half
of the dubious self.
The world was indeed
the anvil stage of fire and ice.
Decades later, balking before
the possibility of a second return
to his ex-wife, the man
would marshal the harvest
of advice counselors had showered—
Try to be compassionate ice
and not foolish fire—but again he'd
stumble onto and become the pyre,
the nest of tinder with words
bursting in grope and spittle.

# MUSTARD SEED MAN

Ballroom tango lessons spoiled the man
to think life tallies up to wisdom. Lean, step,
then a gesture, a shift and an angle,
and lust blossoms up from the floor
into the man's repertoire of easies.
A great bread, as some girl once told him,
is what life is, molded to grow, spill forth
in sunset crusts to lick auroral hungers.
The new wine rending the old skins,
the rich guy squeezing the needle's eye,
everything ached to mount and add and turn
finally into a fabled reserve, the egg
no nest could hold, no chicken would dare.
O but the day he was betrayed
by that woman he had ventured to love,
he understood what the tidal basin taught
glassy with bowled life: an affection
for miniatures. Synecdochic grace
lets the crevice swallow the ocean
of the world. Now, walking
across the decorous park, the man stops to gaze
at the angel's stone lips puckered
in a fountain's floral stage, pouting forth
a stream of crystal. It is no kiss it offers,
but a focusing. She is gone, light and all.

# HANDS-IN-THE-WOUNDS MAN

The man sat in the realtor's office
hoping the latest slump in sales
would garner bargains—palazzos,
he dreamt, for the price of a trailer.
Then the aloof salesman came in
and sat at his desk and turned on
the computer, swiveled the monitor
screen toward the man and clicked away
while greeting him gratingly
through the corners of his mouth and eyes.
This was the virtual tour, the salesman said
routinely, of available houses, click click click,
and the man searched the scroll of images
for his paling dream. He had so wanted
to hop in the salesman's car and visit
houses, stroll through their inhabited
habits exposed to the buyer's silent scrutiny,
imagine himself a ghost planning to live
in the flesh of this space, reversing
the exile of death by closing on a deal.
But virtual tours save gas and time,
and the man could feel his edge
melting away as he touched the screen
on whichever house and said,
This one, this is the one,
this is the one that calls out to me.

# TRANSFIGURATION MAN

To please the new girlfriend the man
climbed the horse, grabbed the reins,
and kicked his heels into the animal
to get him going. Kids and housewives
took the younger steeds, but the man—
being his first time and all—wanted
an easy ride through the Rockies.
Blind in one eye, pissing every ten feet,
the horse he was on fell behind the others
so that soon he was alone
among the aromatic trees and brooks
whose tormented rocks jagged up
like cubist teeth. The trail guide
had turned seeing the man and his horse
locked in their pace and hollered,
"Don't worry, the old guy knows the way back."
The man wasn't sure who he meant,
but there he was atop a beast
who stared into a nearing abyss
cocking his head toward his good left eye,
slipping on pebbles, and just when
the man was sure he would plunge
a thousand mounted feet and die
a newsworthy death, the old guy
turned left and headed back to the stables
where everyone took a deep breath.
The rest of the man's life was filled
with sporadic joys and lasting sorrows,
which made everyone and everything
seem increasingly cellophane-like,
a shimmer, a mist rising from torn water
or a cloud snagged on pine and cliff.

He always wondered if he hadn't
fallen off the cliff with the old stallion
and when would he finally know
how trite these life-in-a-second plot endings
were, or if they were the only ride in town.

# SIN-NO-MORE MAN

Had the man remembered
to bring the coupon, he would have gotten
10% off on the pizza, which is like a free
big slice or a free topping, free sausage
or broccoli, and it would taste
all that more delicious for the free part.
But the taste of the upgrade
would really be more like 30%
better taste on a 10% discount
because that's how the mind
forgives the debt the world incurred
with him at birth when bouncing parents
and smeared nurses let their eyes
sparkle with the unaimed love
such moments beckon. Only later,
they pocketed this love
and the coupon crumpled
like gray dirt a plough has no heart for,
and it curled into a tiny paper fist
fingertips would find in the seam,
fuzzy and pillowed in a mucous doze.

# CAIAPHAS MAN

His lawyer challenged the accuracy
of the radar gun, stressed the bushes
that clearly obscured the cop's view,
the heat burrowing down upon his sweaty eyes.
So the judge tossed the ticket
and the man was happy with the lawyer,
and leaving the courtroom he sneered at the cop
and drove off just over the speed limit
screeching his tires festive
the trial had gone his way and wondering
how anyone gets justly nailed
given how easy it all went.

# WASHING-THE-FEET-OF-THE-POOR MAN

The man was amazed to hear on the science program
that two or three earths could fit inside
that constant storm swirling its sick eye
on Jupiter. Like billiards in a rack,
fingers in a glove, a jogger's scrotum,
comfortable eggs in a hard boil—our earth
and one or two like it coiling in bubbles
in the pot of the tempest, until the pull
of season would make each dutiful world
abandon the carnival of metaphor
and resume its place within the churn of orbit
around, which is to say within,
the typhoon of the sun.

# AGAPE MAN

The man recalled how when he chewed
bubble gum as a boy he was indistinguishedly

desirous of blowing the biggest bubble,
breaking the eyeball records among his buddies,

and doing just that on his birthday once,
and how happy he was to suck the pink skin

of once bubble from his face, how it bearded
there foreshadowingly, and how he wished for once

he'd have the tongue of a toad to sweep
the icky prey from his cheeks with one lick.

He would ponder, by way of a philosophical
exercise much later in a science class,

how many bubble-gum molecules had stayed
invisibly on his face with each burst, thus

eroding the moon of the balloon a measureable
bit with each burst and lick and chew and blow again,

methodical as orbit, or if instead the sucked
tatters of the gum had not picked off molecules

from his face, so that with each turn he'd be less
and the bubble would be more, with bits of him

now bonded to the ever more alabaster expanse
that, in a dream or in the hope of one, would cover

his whole head, laundry-bag him, jellyfish him,
Jonah him down never to emerge again.

# BETHANY MAN

From afar it looks like the bus is stranded
by a field, the tourists mulling about with cameras

and binoculars, waiting for the replacement bus
to take them into town. But actually this is

the place they want to be, empty field only
to empty minds. They gather in stillness

and listen for a special birdsong, or the creak
of a cricket, and train their lenses on where

they think it came from, the wind stirring up
fuzzy seeds from weeds that spring here,

combing then uncombing sprigs
and whipping blooms, a moth cartwheeling

irreparably in the jostle, falling
to waiting beetles, lizards and ants.

They too are on the watch for what feeds them.
They too do not believe in escape.

# FOOL-FOR, SLAVE-FOR MAN

The man finally went to a therapist
to figure why he couldn't let go
of the woman who betrayed him,
so in love was he
with the Nile of plots in which
a meaty ghost met a hungry one
and bones marked the feast
by the shore already so osseously
littered that one morning
while sitting in Concourse D
of Miami International Airport
the man watched a woman
absently drop a candy wrapper
in a trash can but missed,
so she stooped to pick it up
and crumple it and toss it rightly.
Only the man, like a sail filled
with epiphany, rose and walked over
to the can and reached down
and retrieved and straightened the wrapper,
and in front of the bewildered woman
still standing there, let it fall to the floor.
Madame, he said, let things have their way
for all it took to lose and forget
was the opening of your hand
and not the keeping darkness.

# REVELATIONS MAN

The man sat at the airport gate,
and behind him a couple in their forties
chatted about the last minute details
of their vacation. Did you mail
the check? Did you call your mother?
All the man could make out
was the questions. Their responses
to each other were muddled and drowned
out by the noise and background music
the man only now noticed, now that he
caught himself inadvertently informed
while catching ripples of keyboard
and callous horns. The questions, louder,
stabbed through noise like sunlight
between planks of a passing fence.
Another security announcement
and names of standby hopefuls
grabbing a seat in the mind of the flight.
He then heard a few other clearer words
without the bridge of grammar—dog food
dry cleaning wedding cake. Between their
mufflings, the man kept struggling
to string all this into a life he'd captured
winkingly, and more words boarded
the man's sense of sense rising, molding
it all from murk and ash. He had them,
finally, in suspicion and detail,
and could slit the throat of their past
with a plot like the knife of dawn.

## ELIJAH MAN

The man thinks he heard his name
at last, mangled by the gate
attendant, and he snatches the last
standby seat, marveling
it was a window, 27F,
on a clear day, 35 thousand feet
over the Atlantic off Georgia,
facing east, moving north,
and near enough to God's luck
to wonder why no one gets
his name right and why blue and green,
the very colors of nature's expanses,
just don't go well together,
even if today he opted to wear
a blue shirt and green trousers
with a gray jacket and red tie,
still, something's wrong
with the scheme, something
no one else notices
about the quiet man
who always travels alone.

## MILK AND HONEY MAN

The man's flight has him over Virginia,
mica chips of brown and green farming
what the eye surveys, sandy fallows,
ochre roads in the swing and toss
of sudden turbulence. The plentiful
harnessed earth tumbles,
and details locust into blur
in homage to the creatures
no one understands a reason for—
like the rat and the germ—
except as a bravado of number
blotting out daylight and turning
everything into the color
of their clay guts.

# CALLING DISCIPLES MAN

At cocktail parties, perhaps because
his tie usually matched his socks, the man
would often find himself trapped
by tellers of insidious tales,
unsewn and waiting for the flesh
of coherence that never forms.
How, the man's shaking head wondered,
could these fragments lava forth
from contented lips on such flushed
and pitied faces, until he could no longer say
"O my" again. Like any other mantra'd thing,
this one too dimmed from meaning.
And so the man, incapable at last of mercy
for the boring who never get bored,
hobbled to the restroom mirror
and was startled to see his left eyelid
close by itself, without another muscle moving
on his cleaved face, and was rewarded
in his calm when he could do this again
and again, with one eye then the other,
petal gentle, each lid catching a leaf's breeze,
and the two pages of his face now seemed
spined by a new way to escape the fervent
familiars. He ventured out, armed
with his new mitosis, to corner
those who cornered and stare
into their sponging rant. At the right moment
the man closed one eye,
then the other, and the words stopped
and watched to see if the man's eyes took
their freedom seriously, their minds now
the baskets of a secret they were
unsure of deeply wanting.

# GETHSEMANE MAN

Tuesday, 2 a.m., the man stops
at a red light in the snore of suburb,
no cars but his under the red stern,
and he wonders if it might just
be alright to run the light
for he's looked both ways twice now
and the cavern street crickets blindly.
But law is law, and he clutches
the wheel in the eternal unfeeling
stop, when he sees a light coming
on the left, slowly, and this justifies
his waiting in obedience, sitting
in invisible irons. He is ready for joy
when the car slows two blocks away
then turns right, and the man
is now slapped by empty hope,
panged into judging himself
the fool of measure, for truly
there is no one else in sight
or so disposed to weigh
night against night.

# NICODEMUS MAN

Imagine you are a predator
in a nature show on TV,
and your only food is a dying breed,
one of whose members is scrounging
in the snowy earth twenty feet away,
a den of its wrinkled pups waiting nearby,
and you are too hungry to consider
any change in the millennial menu,
and it is then, six feet from your lunge,
that the growl of your empty gut
betrays your position. But the prey
mothers on softly munching,
and it is clear she is deaf
and focused only on her hope,
and cannot notice you until
your jaw clamps and your claw tears,
and it is clear that God, your God,
has answered you.

# GIVE-US-THIS-DAY MAN

Every morning breakfast became
the stage on which pills danced and sang,
assumed the role of hero, were gulped
into the audience of his flesh. As they grew
in number, they fanned into colors and shapes,
textures and sizes. Given the dailiness,
he learned to sniff them into an orchestra,
rolled them on his fingertips to script
a blind menu of their casings. All of which,
he believed, would improve his fading
memory. The short-term was going first
and hardest, and it wouldn't be long
before the very map of his life
sogged into a cereal's milky spectacle,
the juice no longer cold, the coffee
rooming into dullness. Staring out
into his garden, where hummingbirds
lapped the early flowers and stitched
the air with their mechanicals, as if
a great hand was moving them like a cursor
across the screen of a life that remembered
everything, it dawned on him
that his wife, if he had one, could bake him
a memory flan, melding into its lapping moon
the contents of these capsules, so that
he could at least remember, in the throng
of this warm moment, that this caramel host
Petri-dish crown telescope-lens chalice nipple
was the globe, the cage, the very eye and lid
of the one taste that could deny
what lived within it.

# BROKEN SEALS MAN

His flight approaching Charlotte
in 30 mph gusts through jittery clouds
that popped bin latches, the man decides
to find meaning in how farms below
are both like and unlike each other,
of a kind yet shape-betrayed and sized
for difference. Like our names so cleaved,
the first saying this, the last saying them.
In the scroll of dying flight, farms will do
in rock as in peace, for the man is quiet
certain these parcels know measure
and dominion, as do the muscled clouds,
each one call-deserving yet authoring
variance by caught hue and false promontory.
They are like bread slices at the self-service
counter, sandwiched and sandwiching,
locked into a formation that codes
and condemns them. Fizzle, but leave
a mark—so many admonish.
But the sign will remain only if
a kind sees its common mirrored there.

# SCOURGING-AT-THE-PILLAR MAN

Only later did the bonsais become
an obsession. At first, like all sirens,
the draw felt like a drift.
Much eventually did it leap to hunger,
a thirst for smallness
that would not betray its truth.
The decorous tree of mind
held in the painless palm, forcing
the eye to deceive itself like a camera.
A monument to scale in its defiance,
as any man who suffers knows
it doesn't matter if the fault is earned
or it befell him, he cries equally
whatever birth the cause knew,
whatever hand holds the lash
like a branch burning in the ire
of a blind storm.

# ORIGINAL SIN MAN

Embarrassed by the awe he felt
as a boy touching
a mimosa shut
along the vein, tiny leaves
blinking into supplicant palms,
the man came to understand
that astonishment. Beyond
vegetable with a reflex—
didn't venus flytrap also clamp,
and don't sunflowers turn?
He grasped the aesthetics
of mimosa's fruitless act,
effect which refused its turn
to cause. Mimosa stands
reiterative, hence defiant,
its only purpose
to shoo the man away
from botany books which might
disclose a use for mimosa's
sensitivity. He preferred
instead to see in its otherwise
unremarkable nature
a stubbornness worthy
of prophesy.

# MICAH MAN

*[3:5-7]*

Defeated by another universe
show on TV, a dust of stars

poring the x-ray inversions
of a thigh of Milky Way,

the man clambers for similars—
the cobwebs outside his fixed office window

which he exhumes mentally every day
into a widow's locks. It is not true,

he learned online, that hair grows
in the flannel dark. Once shelved,

it is all death and little lights
get bigger in the cloth of flesh,

if you held the corpse up, if you shot it
with brilliance. Like burlap we would be,

thought the man, thick at the feel
but bled with absences everywhere.

That curl of darkness crudding up the heavens
made the man wonder if the web on the pane

would mean anything to him if the spider
had stayed to tidy things up.

## CYMBALS MAN

Repelled by urinals, the man
usually enters a stall, kicks
the manual flush, surveys the idiot
scribbles. He is not alone
in his predilections
for parentheses. Yes, the racket
of his flow resounds
among the face-blind
who pass through, and the point
of porcelain is to be deaf.
At the exact moment
the jellied metallics of his pee
begin to drum, a companion
in the next stall has also commenced.
And it must be occurring to him, too,
the man thinks, how simultaneity
announces each to the other,
both pondering their stream
and parsing the clanging coin
of his splash from the adjacent one,
and wondering if the precision
of the starting line will be met
with the sash of completion snapping
on the twin winners' chests
amid an astronomy of lenses and flashes.
But, the man now muses,
if this is a competition, surely
the champion is he who finishes last,
whose bladder can grip
the weight of the world
much as the better mind can juggle
the copious clauses of numerals

or fan a deck of ideas with a flick.
And what better race than this,
for no trickery can jockey the flow,
and, paged by gray lumber,
each is but a sound to the other,
a presence devoid of man
and therefore parallel to love,
in sparkled purities that forbid
knowledge, envy,
and the hammer of triumph.

## PATMOS MAN

It finally rained, finally,
and the man drove through the shine
of his neighborhood made new
like a prophet through a city
that needed him again.
Just last week the lost dogs
of trash, turned into a pack
by the wind, had leapt onto his windshield
and bit hard on the dust the way
dust can bite. And in the new drip
of the world, the man saw a shivering
dog someone had left out in the yard,
or maybe it always lived like that,
because there's no explaining the cold
eye of the great horde quietly
in the tumult of their days
watching their warm TV
while the world tears.
Much as any other day, the man
tried not to think of his neighbor
who lost his two year old
when his wife ran off one morning
and in the confusion crashed.
The father identified the corpses,
and surely ever since not a leaf
gets pruned, not an appliance is turned off,
not a snail gets egged onto its simplest end,
nothing but nothing passes the natural ledger
without that father sawing himself in half
on the stage in which he is both
magician and the numb assistant,
and he is the audience, too,

and the one who solves the riddle
of how the bright girl
leaps up after the trick,
as if all we ever wanted
from this life was the final leaping
amid cheers in the stab of light,
or, failing that, how to bear
the saw in the thunderous box,
given the long-forbidden why,
now that drought marks
the nature of all seasons.

# AMAZING GRACE MAN

Three in the afternoon. North
on Highway 27, city to his right
and Everglades to the left, thunder
gathering to the north and west,
and amid the flatness, the man
ponders a naked field of melaleuca trunks
blurring the horizon with their spokes.

A clearing in the gray betrays
a moon spooked in blue, spawning
on the tray of heaven like evidence
at a crime scene, the one fingerprint.
The man is glad the invasive plants
are dead or dying so the ground might
recoup the theft of waters. The birds
and all the native croplings, he muses,

will rejoice. How did they die?
Did the experts decipher how to rid
the earth of an invited plague?
Or is it just the call of season,
winter finally wilting before the rains,
and this bleak sight but a swindling hope?
And so, the man figures, the topaz
of clouds, the gusts piling like words,

will restore nothing, feed what kills,
and otherwise ignore in its machinery.
The man tracks the daytime moon
before the system clamps spring down
and knows it foretells, among other things,
tonight's unbending night. He calls ahead,
late again. Better to call so no one worries.

# CONVERSION MAN

Out with the dog and thinking
he should let his mind take in the trees
and the dappling of shadows on pavement
and the rustlings of trash and dryness
so that the walk would feed
the aesthetic impulse his wife's
feng-shui guru had admonished
in that pudding muffled voice,
he let the dog sniff away, heel-free,
and it was then he saw the creature,
a lambent iguana on a rain-inked
oak trunk which the dog's nose too
found magnetic, and as they neared
the reptile slid to the other side,
which made the man gripping the leash
but now focused solely on the apparition,
skulk with his nature-show smile
to the creature's hidden half,
filling with suburban satisfaction,
which made the iguana close its orbit
away from the body of his gaze,
one eye on the man and the other on the dog
marking and marking the trunk in an epistolary
novel of hormones, so the man recalled
another science show about the always
dark side of the moon, and he conjured up
his non-satellite consciousness,
happy the guru's yap was proving useful
as a gust uncombed his thinning hair,
and in this jasmine moment he stamped
his body to the tree, facing east
as his lunar dog, in the first stages of his own

Spartacus mind, leashed the man's legs
to the trunk, and the iguana
watching the canine loops—as the man
in his new mind had prophesied
and driven by his scaly instinctual desire
to be ignored—dawned right up
to the bark-cheeked man, and stared
at him, and the man stared those inches back,
before the reptile figured it was time
to scamper up the tree to where the cradle
of the canopy swayed in a spirited wind.

# MOSES MAN

The man received the first symptoms
of a heart attack, worrying only that at work,
if he dropped to the floor, there would be
sirens and oxygen and the treadmill
of salvation. He watched within his body,
with the fist of senses one has trained
upon oneself, the clench of chest, the brooding
moving pressure not yet pain,
the brick of arm, the spring of needling vessel.
The dizziness and the nascent nausea,
all the foxtrot that led up to the aria
of cobra lightning and iron gate slammed.
He wanted, like a drunk gambler junkie,
to reach his entombing room.
He'd lie, a folded blank page
inside the envelope of nude sheets,
space humming like the neighbor's dryer.
He would settle for nothing short
of nothing and no one. If not, then,
better to mend and resume,
shake off the indigestion and walk
across the ardent quake and up the rabid stairs,
grapple with the wiry boxes inside of wiry boxes,
and stay sand-blind married to the living.

# ADULTERY MAN

When his mother got the news
that a coworker of hers from long ago
had died in a plane crash, she said
to her son, You know,
she would have made a good match
for you, and she always liked you,
except you were married then,
and later, after I left that job,
you were divorced and I forgot
all about her. She sighed
her eyes toward the window,
thankful that sight passes
through the ghost of glass
rather than smashing
into a foggy mountain.
The surprised man said,
I might have saved her
from boarding that plane.
Or, the mother said,
you would have accompanied her.
After all, it's me you send off
on planes alone. It's me
you'll never die with.

## WAGES MAN

So mutation offers new paths, some of which
lead off a cliff and others take you
through the drive-thru and you're
down the timely highway while others
are still humming in line or unwrapping
food that looks better than it tastes. Imagine
an ant who carries a shadow proverbially
ten times its weight, judging its juiciness
for the colony by the shape it casts
on the ant road. A doughnut that will feed us all
for a week or two, months. And when
it finally arrives, the last soldier home,
given the enormity of its find,
they can't let him in. For one thing,
the shape-finder was not a size-considerer,
and even ants know about Troy.
More importantly, the guards at the gate
remind the avid little treasure hunter ant
that the doughnut is made of plastic,
hence its relative lightness and not-relative
inedibility. If it's art, it stays outside.
The hero was stunned, but more importantly,
jettisoned. He lingered about this red thing,
alone. There was no telling his tale
for even he couldn't figure hope into it,
raindrops doming on its surface
beside the white boulders.

# LEPER-NO-MORE MAN

Always enchanted by bridges: suspension
miracles dangling spider highways
or a vaulting cement curve above
the masses of nature. Before planes
taught the eye to move birdly over the earth,
man—the man thought—had bridges.
Even towers are not bird prophetic,
unless it is the perched who are the visionaries,
but that would demand the texts shed
the violent soar of supposition
for the stiff pasture gleaned in the round.
And then the whole thing would have to be
reconfigured, retaught, re-everything,
molt and surmise, like when, in high school
anatomy class, he was stunned and would never
recover upon learning the largest organ
of the body was the skin, seeping and metabolizing,
itching and vasing the man into a shape,
teaching the hidden bones what to hold
and what not to hold onto. The pylons
of calcium, but he, then, was the road,
or the skin was, tracked and vanishing into
a point somewhere within him, vaulted
by bone. So he needed another insight
to calm this one into the flank familiars,
and that's when he learned that leprosy
was not a skin but a nervous-system disorder,
numbing the world of a body into shedding
and wounding, lopping and slashing,
the same nerves, he figured, that dizzied
his gaze from the great bridge, the sea
bearding its slashed snows of crests
as it shoved itself, for now, into the bay.

# GOOD SAMARITAN MAN

The new girlfriend only wept toward the end
of the tale of how her brother, a painter
totally immersed in his work, saved the life
of a friend who tried to help him get recognized.
At first the friend pitied the painter's paralysis
in matters of self-promotion, couldn't land
a gallery, couldn't even find likely galleries
online, so the friend taught the painter these basics
and then wound up doing them himself,
and every other little thing, short of cleaning brushes
and sweeping the studio, until he felt like Jonah
in the belly of someone else's beached life.
So the friend grew distant, but the painter knew
how to track him down, and the friend
quit, changed, ran out of town, and the painter
learned how to find him online, got detective good
in these things. So the friend remembered a story
the painter told him about a man who made
amazing cheeses in Tuscany, the best in the region,
and the painter had figured out it was about
the rocks in the cave where the cheeses were aged,
chemistry, said the painter, and not the skill
of the artisan made the difference, so the friend
found the cheesemaker and became his minion,
did all the menial tasks, because the painter
would never think to look for him here.
But years later—and there's always
a one-day turn in these stories—the painter
walked into the cave, and the friend hid
behind a tower of cheeses, and these, of course,
toppled over and pinned the poor man
who could not even scream for help.

The painter thought about whether to save
the cheesemaker's assistant or pretend
he didn't see him under the wheels of cheese,
and the painter decided to walk away, wheels
turning in his head about how he was going
to dedicate his retrospective to his friend
now that he was the most famous artist in the world.

# CAVE-OF-JEREMIAH MAN

The man walks around a downtown
no one raised in Miami can recognize,
more glass than vanity can stand. The emptier
the condos, the more they shine
like spirits rising in a starry night
sucked back into a black hole.
Figuring out the game one has lost at
is like strip-mining away the gold
to reach the treasure of murk.
Miami has become an empty powder room
for drag queens thumbing a ride out of town.
The man puts his hands in his pocket
because it has gotten a little chilly and he forgot
his cottony sweatshirt. He lights a cigar.
He sees a shadow in one of the balconies
that he supposed universally uninhabited.
Someone is looking right down at him,
also smoking a cigar, hands in his pocket,
inside the yellow wash of a living room
behind a hazy curtain. The man figures
he's projecting again—more therapy,
he guesses, but for what?—
and he suddenly stands still and stares
right up to the shadow 30 floors up,
now leaning on his balcony and staring
right back at the man on the sidewalk.
The guy on the balcony must be waiting
for me to pass before he jumps,
thinks the man. This guy must have been
one of the dupes who bought at the peak
and now, trapped in numbers, he's had it.
But the man can't seem to move, as if he

were naked and his feet were planted
in gelling cement, as in so many dreams
in which people ignoringly circle round
him on their way to work.
But the man feels he is being made real
by the stare from the balcony in the empty tower,
and only that stare can clothe him out of the dream.
Until the guy turns to go back inside,
having finished his cigar, and tosses the butt
to the wind as one might throw
a chewed morsel into a famished multitude
one can't bear to look at.

# JOB MAN

The man imagined himself dreaming
and cast himself as the fifteen-year-old son
of a sculptor spending his vacation at his father's studio
where he works 12 or more hours per day, lugging
wood beams and steel girders in bundles with belts
tied around his neck, and pouring bronze with but rags
to keep from scorching his hands, and welding
without a mask because who knows where the father put it,
and all this in the dank and dark because the electric bill,
and little food, and lukewarm water from a tin can.
The father, meanwhile, supervises the work
from an Eames lounge chair the son bought him
for this very purpose, scrimping from his allowance
and carrying the wondrous object across two time zones
to his father's studio. And as the father rested, he tried
to decipher T'ang poems and Vedic proverbs—
for he fancied himself a learnèd man with many dimensions—
but it was mostly guesswork, though no less fulfilling,
except when the son dropped a hammer and raised
a muscular puff of dust from the floor into a dim gold
seeping from a broken pane, and the father looked up
with muted discomfort and asked the sweaty brute,
Why do you think I am here? And the son wanted to answer,
To make sure I am learning how to become your assistant,
but he was uncertain this was the most obedient answer.
It wasn't, so the father felt compelled to enlighten him:
You are here to experience the worst moment of your life,
so that whatever other horror comes upon you, it will seem
a sweeter fate than this one. This I have done out of love,
that you, my son, may never fear suffering,
for the worst is past, and all else will be a mere imagining.

## DANIEL MAN

The man's boyhood fear of trains—
a string of planets hurtling but aimed—
gave way only in adolescence
when he saw in a movie a tired blonde
getting her feet rubbed by a detective
as she reclined in the yawn of an armchair,
as if, thought the young man, she were
a kite the detective was holding against
a cold front kicking in. Trains, he realized,
were not perilous giants blind,
but, like weather, a condition a coat
or persistence could tame. But last night
he saw a video his artist friend had made
of a train as he drove alongside the seven
freight cars, phone camera perfectly still,
and that's what the man noticed, the steadiness,
until the artist passed the phone
to his stepsister, another artist,
who noticed the marvel of the tree
silhouettes cast by the setting sun
on the dull, graffiti-laden sides of the cars
which the moment had damasked into tidal golds.
The man was baffled he hadn't noticed beauty;
his friend had expected him to notice it.
So, he realized, it wasn't the vast hammer of the train
that terrified him as a boy—even blocks away—
but the ocean he now heard
on the video as an ocean
being set to the music of fire,
and this had always been woman to him,
a single shut eye of moon wounded
and ready to crush or burn or pass on by,
cold, lost.

# LUST-IN-YOUR-HEART MAN

First date. Dinner at a mid-priced eatery.
The man, already finished with his salad,
was still surprisingly interested in this woman,
was not going to pretend someone had called him away
on an emergency. She was probing him,
for interest, in women, reveals itself this way,
and she was curious the man had never been
a father. Don't all men get off on seeing women
pregnant with their seed?, she had always
thought but would never be this blunt.
The fish at this restaurant is particularly
succulent, said the man in a rehearsed monotone,
but the woman still wanted to know. Well,
I was always very careful, said the man.
She looked at him expecting more details.
The man continued: If an avocado rolled off
the basket we were carrying to the truck,
and it splatted on the ground, I never heard about it.
He was pleased he had come up with such an agrarian
motif, but the woman just then swallowing the last
piece of avocado in her salad, looked wistfully at the plate,
bidding this fruit that is always taken for a vegetable
adieu. How could she eat avocado ever again
and not think of a sexual disaster? Misreading
the pause, the man went on, dazzling her no doubt
with tropes. If I nearly choked on a plum pit, if I
ate a salmon skin and all, if I buried my face
in rice pudding . . . no one ever. . . .
She said nothing, for this, she knew
was more than love.
This is a man she could live with
and lose weight at the same time.

# NO-RECORD-OF-WRONGS MAN

Why suddenly were childhood memories
backing up onto the lawn of the man's mind,
like this one at the interstate diner as he poured
sugar in his styrofoam coffee? When he was 13,
his best friend's mom had gone on a trip
to Europe. Her first in ages, despite
her wealth. Longtime a widow,
she, her mother, and her youngest son
lived behind the man's family's
far more modest house. The man
at the time spent countless hours
at his friend's. Porcelains and jades,
all the Louis in carpets and fans,
chandeliers and furniture. Ivories, crystals.
And diamonds in constellations on her fingers.
The garden, too, tumbled with flowers
and perfumes, a weeping willow, and myriad
odd-leafed shrubs, all of which the lady
tended to with fanatical grace, gloved
and wide straw hat ribboned at the chin.
A slender, short woman with a submarine
clarity in her eyes, the stare at times of a statue,
who tied teabags to her enormous gardenia
and azalea bushes that the acids might suckle them.
Blue herons would nest in their ten towering
eucalyptus trees. The lawn shoed your shoes
when you walked on it. Every bush had its
own music for the common wind.
She drove a milk-colored Lincoln Continental
with black leather interior. The grandmother,
Boston Irish and simultaneously a down-to-earth
woman and a grand lady, would appear

in luminous portraits the man would later see
in 19th century galleries of museums. Forever
these would be, for the man, echoes of the mansion
in which he became familiar for the first time
with the sensuality of abundance. Not just wealth,
the adolescent would understand,
but a condition of haremic languid joy
from senses spilling with beauty in the hug
of the metronome hearth. And, furthermore,
this eros of transcendent nows ordains
the frequency of mind requisite for civilization.
So, when the lady returned from Europe
and told him she had brought him a special present,
the young man was titillated. She took
a small object from her purse and presented
her oddball son's best buddy with a sugar cube
from the Eiffel Tower, neatly wrapped in burgundy
paper. A tiny sucre written in white on it.
The waitress at the diner asked if he wanted
anything with his coffee. A croissant, he said.
Make that two. Like the many he's had
in a Paris whose Babel he never climbed.

# GOOD NEWS MAN

At first the man was happy if the new girlfriend
was happy—as when he showed her picture on his phone
to friends and they would all say *Wow*. But he soon realized
their exclamations were filled with slicing astonishment,
incredulity that this man should have nabbed a woman
as attractive as that. He came to detest these growling
hurtful Wows that damned even as they pretended
to celebrate his good fortune. She doesn't look that old,
many would say, when he told them she was 50.
Worst of all were the pictures of them together
which left no doubt in most minds that the man
was incredibly rich and had kept this hidden,
for how else to explain this romance.
And with gentle cues, the man learned to garden
that conclusion. He monitored the interlocutor
for signs that indicated marketability of the ruse.
When he adroitly complained that she wasn't accepting
his presents, it didn't work. A feigned annoyance
over her trumped-up extravagances was convincing.
And so with other tested signs that cast him
in the role of a rich tightwad and her in the role
of a joie-de-vivre champ.
Everyone was rooting for her now,
for surely she could free him up,
get him to upgrade from that Honda,
buy better clothes, and all this made him feel
like a man of power, heroically envied,
the man she almost deserved.

## KEPHAS MAN

The man is with his best friend
from college, in Colorado,
driving through fossil fields,
gawking at lithified tree trunks,
and finally coming to South Park,
a seabed hoisted by nature's horns
into the sky. It retains the maritime,
mountains in the distance shoring
what once lay upon the waist
of the world. The two men
walk through the absent tides
in a dust that once thronged dark
with all the giants of the sea
that mirrored the giants of the land,
and who've left behind their shrapnel
on the clean tabletop of this punished earth
like a miserly tip. The man's friend
lives in these parts, but the man
is on vacation, and so he alone
can imagine himself swimming
as he walks, more like a laser point
in a lecture on life immemorial
dragged across, then back, up, down,
proving to the audience he lugs
within his cavernous soul
that water can indeed be hewn
by blows from the rock of ages,
for all men owe themselves
a stab at the granite condition,
whether it be by dream or conviction,
or mere stubbornness.

# GOD-IS-LOVE MAN

The corner bakery opens at 7, fills
with breakfast hawks, overdressed
office types who never figure time
for making coffee and warming
buns, cleaning up, and being
a loving sun of a family person
in the morning, the most delicate time
of the day, when tempers were most likely
to slash and swipe. Why would that be,
the man wondered, that morning tended
to boil people just so? The yank from sleep,
the broken chapter of a dream,
the realization of just how cheap memory
and imagining can be bought—a kiss,
a shower, a swift hump before a day
of duties descends—all these are bribes,
and it is then, the man realized,
that we gather the stones with which
to pelt ourselves, wretches, adulterers
of our kiss to ourselves. Morning
was indeed the proper time to sacrifice
the crumpled lamb, when the sun
might just as well be setting,
and the toll of withering is felt
simultaneously as dawn and twilight.
And who might rise from the desert
of the clean table, and what face might
shape the steam above the styrofoam,
and what bug will think the crumbs
on the floor of the bakery a delivery
from God? Will the man, then,
his number finally called, the last

almond pastry within his reach,
settle for the timed quiet of a corner
broken only by the flocking
of flakes on his lapel, or will
he accept the bread and shoes
of forgiveness?

## GOD-IS-TRUTH MAN

The artist who had been his friend
and who killed himself just
as stardom neared, left no note
or reason. Six years later, a girlfriend
of the artist emails the man,
curious about details of her lover's
demise. They spoke on the phone.
She had long ago rebuilt the pattern
of her life, but obviously still loved.
Make sense, something told her,
make sense of this which others
brush off with awes and pities.
And what of his great work
lingering in a punctual dust
no future could forgive?
How exactly?—the man was surprised
no one had told her, to spare her
the blunt rope and the bag
of the artist's silhouette
dangling in meals of dreams, ripe regret.
So he told her, and she stayed calm.
And he buried his gratitude to the artist
for leaving no note to her or to him,
or even to himself, to anyone who merited
a gentle shove into the slow lava
that laments the sea. For that
is memory. No point in having a point
in the landscape that forbids
the vapid sighs he'll feast on,
the man hopes, in the life to come.

# GOD-IS-LIGHT MAN

*Who will be moved by the sincerity*
*Of my vain day-and-night prayer?*
—Zhang Jiuling, "Thoughts III"

The man walks, smokes the January
out of him. Manhattan in the park
he imagines, a woman friend

has sat herself down, broke,
abandoned by a lover who stole
her inheritance, phone

on its last minutes, she will wait
to die there, cheaply, hidden
from valiant rescue,

as it should be. In the last minutes—
he reads online—of someone dying
in the cold, the person feels

a sudden fire, the body rebelling
against desire. She will soon
rip her clothes off, stagger

in white, a Salomé moment
with veils burning from the baldness
of her lips. The man wraps

his wool lapels tighter in his gait,
no free cab in sight,
the bone-flaked deafness ashing.

What if the storm knocked
out power, the man muses,
and a guy delivering a cake

gets stuck in an elevator
in what seemed like days,
alone, although when the doors

are broken open it was only
a couple of hours, but locked
in hover the landscape stretches

and he senses the storied void
beneath him and ponders if it is right
to eat the cake, for that's all there is,

duty having been jolted onto other tracks,
and though he can't share, it is a crime
to waste food, and alone he cannot

test the reason of his fears
against another. Isn't it like
the way the man had once thought

of art as a stone falling from a great
height, its shadow widening as the stone
neared the ground like a wooly lens,

even as the speed and line of the fall
were steady? Wasn't the life of art,
greedily abandoning its maker,

like that stone, the canvas or page
or ears on which it would eventually land
clouding up at times, edging at others?

Wasn't it like the last gulp in the elevator
as the delivery guy hears the metal scrapes
of rescuers, or the friend in her park

finding the afterlife was not
a T'ang scroll of golden branches
firing invisible arrows of insight

over the heads of pilgrims, landing
on the blurred horizon they are headed for,
a place that will become clear as a rock?

# Recent titles in the Carnegie Mellon Poetry Series

*That Was Oasis*, Michael McFee
*Blue Rust*, Joseph Millar
*Spitshine*, Anne Marie Rooney
*Civil Twilight*, Margot Schilpp

2013
*Oregon*, Henry Carlile
*Selvage*, Donna Johnson
*At the Autopsy of Vaslav Nijinksy*, Bridget Lowe
*Silvertone*, Dzvinia Orlowsky
*Fibonacci Batman: New & Selected Poems (1991-2011)*,
    Maureen Seaton
*When We Were Cherished*, Eve Shelnutt
*The Fortunate Era*, Arthur Smith
*Birds of the Air*, David Yezzi

2014
*Night Bus to the Afterlife*, Peter Cooley
*Alexandria*, Jasmine Bailey
*Dear Gravity*, Gregory Djanikian
*Pretenders*, Jeff Friedman
*How I Went Red*, Maggie Glover
*All That Might Be Done*, Samuel Green
*Man*, Ricardo Pau-Llosa
*The Wingless*, Cecilia Llompart